A WORLD OF DESERTS

Contents

by Kathryn Harper

CAMBRIDGE
UNIVERSITY PRESS

UCL
Institute of Education

A VERY DRY PLACE

Deserts can be hot in the day and cold at night. They can be beautiful but harsh. They can look empty, but there is life.

Something that all deserts have in common is that they are very dry. It can rain in a desert, but the water doesn't stay long. In a desert, more rain **evaporates** than falls.

It has not rained in parts of the Atacama desert for 500 years.

Deserts get less than 25 centimetres of rain in one year. In other places, the same amount of rain can fall in just one hour, in an extreme storm. For example, 30.5cm of rain fell in just 42 minutes in Missouri, USA in 1947.

DESERT SAND

Over thousands of years, the changes in **temperature** can help to break down rocks into very, very small pieces. That's how desert sand is made.

Sometimes, the strong desert wind can blow the sand into piles, called **dunes**. Sand dunes can be very big and very long.

These sand dunes are in the Sahara desert.

3

DESERTS IN THE WORLD

A lot of the land on Earth is desert. People often think of deserts being in hot places. That isn't always true. There are deserts on every continent. They can be in hot places and cold places.

Erg Chebbi, Morocco ⟶

Sonora, USA and Mexico ⟶

KEY
- ○ Sub-tropical
- ● Cold and Polar
- ● Cool coastal and cold winter

Atacama, Chile ⟶

Namib, Namibia

Gobi, China
and Mongolia

Taklamakan, China

Thar, India and Pakistan

ahara

Arabian

Australian

Antarctic

5

DIFFERENT KINDS OF DESERTS

Some deserts are very cold all the time.
The Antarctic is the biggest desert in the world.
It is covered with a thin layer of snow, but it
does not actually snow often.
The little amount of snow that does fall does
not evaporate.

Snow and ice cover the ground, but the Antarctic is very dry.

6

Many deserts are in very hot countries, such as Algeria, Yemen or India.

The Namib is the oldest desert in the world.

Some deserts, like the Namib, are on **coasts** beside oceans. Sometimes they are cooler than hot deserts but they are still very dry. The Namib Desert stretches for 2000 kilometres on Africa's Atlantic coast.

ANIMALS IN THE DESERT

Animals need water, so living in the desert can be difficult for them. Desert animals have special ways of keeping water and food. They also have ways of protecting themselves from the extreme weather and desert conditions.

Camels have **humps** on their backs. These are full of fat. Camels use this fat for food and water. It can last for many days.

The camels' long eyelashes and closable noses help to protect them from sand. Their wide feet stop them from sinking into the sand.

camels walking in the Taklamakan desert

The Australian thorny devil drinks in water through its **skin**.

The South American peccary's mouth is so **tough** that it can eat a **cactus**.

9

The sidewinder rattlesnake moves **sideways**.
This helps it travel over sand without slipping.
Only two points of its body touch the hot sand
at any time.

*This sidewinder
is travelling quickly
over the hot sand.*

The fennec fox has large ears to help it keep cool. They also help to listen out for the insects the foxes like to eat.

a fennec fox

DESERT PLANTS

When there is little water, or if it evaporates quickly, it can be difficult for plants to grow. Desert plants have **adapted** in special ways. Many desert plants have thick, waxy leaves that stop the water inside from evaporating,

Cactus plants **store** water. There are many different sizes and shapes of cactus but they all have spikes instead of leaves.

Palm trees grow in many deserts. The spiny leaves of the palm tree stop camels from eating them. They store **moisture** and **nutrition** in their long trunks.

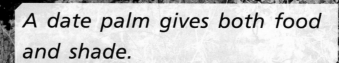

A date palm gives both food and shade.

The Sonora desert has cacti which can reach the height of four giraffes.

13

LIVING IN THE DESERT IN THE PAST

Traditional desert people needed to keep moving to find water and feed their animals.

a yurt

The Bedouin children in the Saharan and Arabian deserts lived in tents with their families. These tents protected them from wind, sun, heat and cold.

Traditional **nomad** children of the Gobi desert lived in round **yurts** with their families. The yurts were made of animal **fur** and skin.

Traditional Bedouin tents were made of goat hair.

LIVING IN THE DESERT TODAY

Today, a few people still live in traditional tents and yurts but most desert people live in modern buildings. They can live in tall apartment buildings or single houses. Their homes and schools often have **air conditioning** to keep them cool.

apartment buildings in Dubai

15

DUST AND SAND STORMS

Strong desert winds cause sand and **dust** storms. These can blow up very quickly. The sand is blown into the air, making huge clouds up to 305 metres high. Dust from a sand storm can travel across oceans.

a sandstorm in Dubai

It's hard to see or even breathe in a sandstorm.
Sandstorms can damage cars, buses and farms.

WATER IN THE DESERT

Most of the desert is dry but sometimes people can find a place with water. This is called an oasis. The water usually comes from **springs** deep under the ground. Many plants and trees grow around it.

an oasis

18

The oasis is an important place where desert people can get water and food. Oases can be very big. Some people build houses and farms around them.

This is the biggest oasis in the world.

THE FUTURE OF THE DESERT

The world is getting hotter and, in many places, deserts are getting bigger. This means that there is less good land for growing food. Many people are going hungry. In some places, **desertification** causes famine.

*This used to be a farm.
Now the desert is taking over.*

In other places, people are learning to work with the desert. Huge **solar farms** use the sun's energy to make electricity. **Wind farms** are also being built in deserts.

The largest solar farm in the world is in Dubai.

This wind farm is in the Thar desert.

Deserts are amazing and extreme places. They give people both challenges and hope for the future.

GLOSSARY

adapted changed to survive in different places

air conditioning system keeping buildings and cars cool

cactus desert plant that can survive hot, dry climates

desertification way that land changes into desert

dunes large piles of sand, blown by the wind

dust small, dry bits in the air and on land

evaporates turns from liquid into steam in the air

fur hair that grows on animals' bodies

humps large lumps on an animal's back

moisture wetness

nomad person who travels most of the time and doesn't live in one place

nutrition food

sideways movement to the side

solar farms large areas that make electricity from the sun

springs places where water comes up from the ground

store collect to keep for some time

temperature scale by which heat is measured

tough strong and hard to break

traditional done in a certain, often old, way

wind farms large areas that make electricity from the wind

yurt round tent

INDEX

A WORLD OF DESERTS ❧ KATHRYN HARPER

Teaching notes written by Glen Franklin and Sue Bodman

Using this book

Developing reading comprehension

This non-chronological report details many interesting facts about deserts. Non-fiction features, such as a glossary, index, maps and charts, support children to practise and consolidate reading for information skills. Whilst the language structures are in the main simple and direct, the topic specific vocabulary and the concepts will be a challenge to the young reader at Gold Band without specific support. Covering a range of distinct aspects (geology, animal colonisation, human habitation), this book offers scope for older children reading at Gold Band to read at their interest level and to develop skimming and scanning skills to locate information.

Grammar and sentence structure

- Sentences are written in a clear, non-chronological report style: generic subject and present tense ('Deserts can be...'; 'Animals need ...', 'desert people live ...').

- Commas punctuate sentences with dependent (subordinate) clauses, such as 'When there is little water, it can be difficult for plants to grow' (p.12).

- Captions and labels are appropriately punctuated.

Word meaning and spelling

- Vocabulary is often technical and specific place names are used.

- Novel or unfamiliar vocabulary is explained in the glossary ('desertification' on p.20), or supported by the illustrations.

- Knowledge of morphological units (such as 'ure', 'tion' and 'al') is used to read multisyllabic words.

Curriculum links

Geography – There are many different deserts introduced in the book. Children could use source material and websites to explore one desert in depth.

Science – Experiment with water and condensation by placing well-watered plants under plastic and seeing how water droplets form. This is one way in which water is created in the desert.

Learning Outcomes

Children can:

- scan the text to find particular sections to locate specific information

- solve most unfamiliar words on-the-run, attending to less common digraphs

- critically evaluate the information given in content and presentation.

A guided reading lesson

Book Introduction

Give a copy of the book to each child. Ask them to read the title and the blurb independently. Discuss what children know already about deserts. For younger children, the book will be useful if linked to a class topic that has already introduced the vocabulary and concepts that will be novel.

Orientation

Ask: *What might you want to find out from reading a book about deserts?* List some of their questions on a board for later reference. 'Are there deserts all over the world?'

Preparation

Ask the children to go to pages 4 and 5. Guide them to interpret the key on page 4. Then go through each colour of the key in turn and locate the areas and places on the map. Read the names of the countries and places aloud a few times and encourage the children to rehearse saying them aloud. (Please note: If children hesitate or make errors with these place names as they read, provide them quickly so that they can read on, maintaining the sense. The places names are for interest and in general do not follow English orthography. This makes them unhelpful for focused teaching of letter-sound relationships.)

Ask the children to look through the book to identify the key features of non-fiction texts: note the use of photographs and captions, maps, index and glossary. Remind the children that non-fiction texts are read differently to story books, in order to locate specific information: *You have thought of some questions you want to answer by reading this book. Let's check how you might find out the answer.*